CW00411285

Parents' Guide to
Pre-School
Education

Roy Blatchford and George Crowther

Contents

Chapter one

Why is education so important in your child's early years?

Millions of words of research, not to mention plain common sense, tell us that parents are truly their child's first and most important teachers. Where do children learn first but with parents – listening, watching, playing and copying. It is the quality of these early years which will determine your child's educational success in the future.

Your child has been learning from the very minute he or she was born. It is often said that half of what we shall ever know as mature adults has been learned by the age of three. So, what has your child been learning?

Social skills

Your child has been learning how to live in a family. How to get your attention when it is needed ... and sometimes when it is not! How to respond to a range of adults and other children. How to please, and how to annoy. A whole range of understanding and skills which shape your child's place in the social world.

Physical skills

Your child has been learning how to be mobile: from crawling and first steps, to walking, running and maybe even swimming. He or she has gradually become more independent concerning where to go and when.

Knowledge

Your child knows a lot about his or her immediate world, home and family, and is beginning to piece together knowledge of the wider world, through outings and books. How many of us have a special event as our very first memory of childhood?

Communication

Your child has gradually learned to communicate with others: at first through cries, later through gesture and facial expression, and eventually through speech, which grows and develops with every day.

Understanding

Your child has learned to understand many things and is expanding his or her knowledge all the time, but that understanding is often incomplete. For example, your child understands about day and night, but in the context of his or her daily routine rather than the motion of the planets. Your child understands the difference between right and wrong, but based on his or her own experience rather than a wider knowledge of justice.

In all these ways, your child is beginning to make sense of his or her world. Parents need to be aware of how far their child has progressed down each of these pathways, so that they can provide the next steps in learning. Extending and developing your child's skills, knowledge and understanding is the real challenge of being a parent.

Chapter two

What difference can parents make?

Playing your part

Parents can, and do, make a difference to their child's early education. All research shows that parents who provide the right experiences for their child, and encourage their child to succeed, make a significant impact on early learning. So what should parents do?

Talk to your child

This sounds so obvious, but have you considered the range of talk in which you engage your child? So often, because of the pressures of family life, most of our talk with our children is routine. How often do we really discuss something of interest with them? How often do we discuss feelings and emotions? How often do we encourage them to speak at greater length?

Extending the range of your child's language should be your aim in the early years, challenging them to use new words and express their ideas in different ways. Don't be afraid to use 'big' words – children often remember them. Don't shy away from asking awkward questions – they get the brain working. Take opportunities when you are in new and different situations to extend your child's vocabulary. It is important for children to know the correct words for objects, rather than just the 'baby' words.

Day trips and outings

A visit to Aunt Ann is just as valuable as a day at Alton Towers. It is not the distance, or the price, it is the variety of settings in which you place your child which will develop his or her skills. If there is a new environment to explore, if there are new people to meet, if there are new rules to understand, your child will be expanding a range of skills. Remember to make the most of every opportunity and really observe your child in a new setting to learn more about what he or she can do. This does not have to mean that you carry a checklist of things to do with your child every time you go out. Keep it natural and spontaneous and remember that it's just as important that you enjoy yourself as it is that your child does.

> 'Excellence can be achieved only on the basis of partnership. We all need to be involved: schools, teachers and parents are at the heart of it. We also need the help of all of you: families and the wider community. We need your commitment if we are to get our children off to a good start. Everyone has a part to play.'
>
> *from the foreword to* The White Paper on Education *David Blunket, Secretary of State for Education (DfEE, 1998)*

Involving your child

So often we miss opportunities to involve our children in different activities because, if we are honest, we know that it will take longer for us to complete them. Whether it is baking, washing-up, cleaning the car, wiring a plug – any household job – if your child is interested, they will learn from the experience. And it creates lots of opportunities for different types of talk. If your child chooses the bananas at the supermarket or helps you bake a Christmas cake it takes a little longer, but they learn more in the long run.

Reading

It is really rewarding and worthwhile to read to your child – the vast majority of children are fascinated by stories and enjoy the close, secure feeling of reading with an adult. Try to choose good quality books, from the shop or library, which have stories and characters which will appeal to your child. Look for books with interesting illustrations to explore. As well as encouraging your child to love books, you will be teaching him or her many early reading skills about turning pages, the way print relates to the pictures, and using expression in your voice.

Young children soon develop favourite books, and often will not allow you to miss out even one page, or word, from a book they know really well. Again, reading books creates a different setting for developing talk. Remember that children need to see their parents enjoying reading, so they come to see it as a worthwhile activity.

Games

Play games with your child – even simple games can help to develop the range of children's skills, and this is why playgroups, pre-school groups and nurseries usually adopt a 'play' approach. However, if play has no structure, then learning may also be limited. Whether you play with a bat and ball, dominoes or jigsaws, try to teach your child the best way to do it. In other words, include some teaching alongside your enthusiasm and encouragement.

Try to make sure that your child has a range of toys and games, from simple construction kits to soft toys, to encourage a range of play. Young children often prefer solitary play, but try to encourage sharing with a friend because this will be important for them later in life.

Television

Monitor television viewing – be in charge of how much, how often and what your child watches. Use television and videos to stimulate talk, rather than as an excuse for some peace and quiet. Listening to radio and cassettes also helps your child's listening skills and concentration.

The difference you can make to the quality of your child's early learning should never be under-estimated. All experiences are important, and parents can positively influence the pattern of their child's life, as well as how much they derive from each experience.

Chapter three

Your choices for pre-school education

There is a range of opportunities for your child's pre-school education. The two main providers of pre-school education are playgroups and nurseries. Playgroups offer early learning experiences in an informal setting and parents are often involved in running the sessions. Nursery is a more formal place where a teacher will organise children's learning. Many nurseries are attached to schools.

Playgroups

Many parents choose to send their children to playgroups, family centres or toddler groups, where they feel their child will encounter new people and experiences. The principle advantages for your child are:

– the opportunity to experience a wide range of activities which extend the ones you are able to offer in the home

– the opportunity to play alongside and with a variety of children

– the opportunity to meet and interact with a range of adults

There are also advantages for parents, because they meet other parents and can enjoy a varied social life.

There may be a range of early learning groups in your area. How can you choose the best setting for your child? Here are some points to consider:

▶ Are the staff warm and welcoming to you and your child?

▶ Is the room/area well organised? Does it allow for children (and adults) to move around freely between activities? Are there places for parents to sit? Do the activities look 'used' (which is their purpose) but not a mess?

▶ Does the playgroup offer a wide range of activities for children? Look for:

– lots of interesting books and a comfortable place to read

– drawing and mark making, with a range of pencils, crayons and papers

– painting and printing

– cutting and sticking

– water play and sand play

– playdough, Plasticine or clay

– building and constructing

– a creative play area – maybe a house, Post Office or hospital

– jigsaws and games

– singing sessions and music making

Good playgroups will have given much thought to this range of activities because they want to provide opportunities for children to develop their full range of skills.

Other areas to consider include:

▶ How many staff are there per child? If the playgroup caters for many children and there are few staff, it is likely that your child will receive less attention.

▶ Do the staff relate well to the children whilst they are working? Watch the staff when they work with the children: are they helping children to learn through their play?

▶ Is your child happy in the setting? This is probably the most important factor for parents, but don't forget to ask yourself if your child will be engaged in constructive activities.

Nurseries

Nursery education is often the next step for children, before they begin primary school. Nurseries will usually be for slightly older children and, unlike playgroups, parents will not normally stay with their child during the sessions. However, it is quite common for nurseries to welcome parents as helpers, on a rather more formal basis than playgroups.

Why is nursery different from playgroup?

Like playgroup, nursery aims to widen your child's experience by providing a range of learning situations. It should also provide an increasingly structured set of experiences which build on your child's existing skills. Above all, nursery aims to support and encourage your child's ability to learn.

Learning how to learn

There should be opportunities to work with, and learn alongside, a range of adults and other children, building the important skills of co-operation and interaction. There should be opportunities to work individually, with increasing concentration, so that your child can learn to focus on an activity. There should be lots of opportunities for success and satisfaction in a task which has been completed well, building your child's confidence in his or her own ability.

Encouraging a range of learning

Nurseries aim to provide a wide range of learning experiences. There should be opportunities for:

– your child to listen to and enjoy stories and to begin to understand how print and books convey a meaning: these experiences will support your child when he or she begins to read independently

– creative activities with paint, music, modelling and drama

– dealing with numbers, patterns and shapes which will support later development in mathematics

Good nurseries provide more structure for your child's learning.

All these experiences will enrich your child's learning and introduce him or her to new interests. In a good nursery school, the teachers make sure that each child receives a balanced diet of activities, and that every child's talents are successfully built upon.

Preparation for the next stage of education

Nurseries value and provide a particular style of education which is appropriate for young children, based on play with a clear learning purpose. They also recognise that they are preparing children for the next stage in their education, and the more formal demands of primary school. In good nursery schools the teachers are aware of the next steps which children will be taking. They aim to develop the knowledge and skills which will enable your child to make a smooth start at primary school.

The debate about nursery education

Nursery education has been catapulted to the top of the political agenda by a series of events. The offering of Nursery Vouchers for four year olds, on a trial basis in some parts of the country in 1996, and then nationwide in 1997, attempted to ensure that all parents could afford good quality nursery education for their child. This led to a boom in nursery places, both in the state and private sector, and in places offered for four year olds in reception classes in primary schools. This funding-led expansion did not always produce good quality facilities, with many primary schools in particular being criticised for the poor quality facilities they offered to their youngest children.

Nursery vouchers were then phased out by the Labour government in 1997, but it is still committed to providing a nursery place for every four year old. The recent government document, *Excellence in Schools,* emphasises the importance of nursery education:

> *'We know that children who benefit from nursery education are more likely to succeed in primary school. Indeed, the quality of children's pre-school and primary education has been shown to have a major impact on their achievements at 16 and their wider social skills.'*
>
> *from* Excellence in Schools *(DfEE, July 1997)*

Why does everyone think that nursery education is so important?

The evidence for the importance of nursery education comes from long term studies in the USA. Special programmes set up in the 1960s, in the poorest areas of many cities, offered good quality nursery education to selected children. This was called the Headstart project. The progress of these children has been tracked over the last 30 years. It has been shown that, compared with children who did not benefit from nursery education, these children have been more successful educationally, are more likely to be in higher paid employment and are less likely to have been involved in criminal activities. It is solid evidence to prove something which parents have known for a long time. Nursery education is important.

How can you make the most of the nursery education opportunities which are available in your village, town or city? The following pages aim to help you through the decisions which you might make about your child's nursery education.

What is nursery education?

Parents can be forgiven for being confused about nursery education. Is the converted house at the end of the street a nursery? Is the provision at the local school a nursery, a reception class or an early years' unit? Now that there are no Nursery Vouchers, do parents have to pay for a nursery place? The whole subject of nursery choices has become very complicated, and the confusion grows.

The reality is that there is a wide range of provision which calls itself nursery education, and it falls into two distinct types.

State nursery school

▶ Free.

▶ Often attached to a primary school, but may be a separate nursery school serving a range of primary schools.

▶ Offers places to three and four year old children, depending on the local policy and demand.

▶ Offers two separate sessions, morning or afternoon, Monday to Friday. Your child may be offered a choice of session but, because there is often high demand for places, you may have to accept either.

▶ Each session must be 2.5 hours.

▶ Most commonly 26 children attend each session, but there may be more or fewer.

▶ For 26 children, at each session the staff must consist of a qualified teacher and a trained assistant (often holding an NNEB qualification – see page 14) at least. There should be more if the number of children is increased.

Children from the local community (possibly the primary school's catchment area) will have priority for admission, but you should be able to obtain a copy of the nursery school's admission policy which will provide details.

For example:

Brookside Primary School, Bicester, Oxfordshire

Brookside Primary School has a nursery class as part of its provision. The nursery occupies a separate, purpose-built building, with spacious indoor and outdoor work and play areas. The nursery teacher is a qualified primary teacher, who has considerable experience working with nursery age and reception children. She works alongside a nursery assistant who holds an NNEB qualification. The nursery offers 52 places, 26 for the morning session and 26 for the afternoon. The sessions operate within school time only.

Most of the children who attend the nursery live near the school. Some will then go on to attend Brookside Primary School and some will attend St Edburg's CE Primary School, which is also local to the nursery. The two schools work jointly to provide nursery education for their pre-school children. A few places are reserved for children with special needs.

▶ Fee paying. Charges will vary, depending on the hours you wish your child to attend.

▶ Not affiliated to any particular primary school.

▶ Offers longer hours of opening, and child care to meet the needs of working parents.

▶ Takes children from an early age until they start school.

▶ Should have sufficient staffing to meet the needs of the children. Currently the ratios are:

2-3 year olds: 2 staff to 8 children

3-5 year olds: 1 staff to 8 children

▶ May draw children from a wide geographical area and take new children as places become available.

For example:

Dinky-Doo Nursery, Oxford

Dinky-Doo is a small independent nursery, situated in a large, converted house in the suburbs of Oxford, which has an extensive garden for outdoor activities. It has been established for 12 years and is run by a principal and a trained NNEB and teacher. It caters for children between the ages of two and five years, and aims to prepare children for pre-prep school. Most of the children who attend live within a three mile radius of the nursery, but some come from further afield.

It operates from 8.30am to 5.00pm, Monday to Friday, throughout the year, and after school facilities are available for parents until 5.30pm. The nursery is fee paying, and the current charges range from £91.00 for a full week to £12.50 for a morning session only.

There are many nursery schools which offer a combination of the provision outlined above. For example, there are state nursery schools which offer elements of child care, but their primary purpose remains educational. Private nurseries, whilst providing a service for working parents, will also aim to provide high quality educational experiences for the children. The rest of this book covers mainly nursery education, but is also useful for information about playgroups.

Chapter four

Choosing a nursery for your child

Finding out about nurseries in your area

Your Local Education Authority (LEA) will be able to provide brief details of the state nursery schools in your area which should include the name and address of the nursery, the headteacher's name, and information about the capacity of the nursery.

Your local Social Services department will be able to provide brief details of the private nurseries in your area, because it is responsible for inspecting the quality of childcare provision. In both cases, a telephone call should be sufficient to obtain this information.

Do not forget to ask other parents with young children, particularly if you are new to an area, because their opinions may well be a good starting point in seeking a nursery. Health visitors will also know about local nursery provision.

Checklist for assessing nursery brochures

Each nursery or nursery school should have a leaflet or brochure which gives factual details about the nursery and also outlines some of the educational principles which the staff of the nursery feel are important. Again, a telephone call should secure a copy of this document. It is well worth reading the information about any nursery you are considering for your child.

Here is a brief checklist which will help you to judge the information you read in a nursery school brochure.

> ▶ Is the brochure presented in an attractive, thoughtful and accessible way?

> ▶ Does it tell you what you want to know?

> ▶ Does it tell you what the nursery aims to achieve with your child?

> ▶ Does it tell you about staff qualifications and the roles of the staff?

> ▶ What does it tell you about the range of activities offered?

> ▶ What does it tell you about support for individual children?

> ▶ Does it tell you how you will be kept informed about your child's progress?

> ▶ Does it tell you how you can be involved in the work of the nursery? Is there an active parents' association to support the nursery?

Visiting nurseries

Reading the documents from each nursery in your area should help you to begin to decide which of the nurseries will best meet the needs of your child or, at least, help you to narrow down the possibilities. Distance from home to nursery and travel arrangements may also be decisive.

When you feel confident that you have selected the best options, it is important that you visit the nurseries. Documentation may be glossy and glowing, but what does the nursery look like in operation? When you contact the nursery to arrange a visit, try to ensure that you are visiting on a normal morning or afternoon session, and that you can arrive at the beginning of the session: this will give you the best possible opportunity to judge the quality of the nursery.

You need to make a decision about whether to visit a nursery with or without your child. Many parents choose to take their child on the visit, and this has the advantage of seeing how your child reacts in the situation. However, the danger is that you will not see some of the things which are going on in the nursery because you have to respond to the needs of your own child. You will know the best approach, but it is best to be aware of the advantages of each.

Here is a checklist which will help you to judge the quality of the nursery during your visit. Watch the children carefully because they are the best indication of whether the nursery is providing good quality experiences.

Checklist for your first visit to a nursery

► Are you made to feel welcome when you arrive at the nursery?

► Do other parents, arriving with their children, appear to be happy and 'at home' in the nursery? Ask them what they like about the nursery and why they chose it.

► Do the children arrive happily to start their session in the nursery? Are staff ready to welcome them and deal with their needs?

► Is the nursery environment attractive and inviting? Are there plenty of examples of the children's work on display?

► Do the children know the routines which have been established? For example, children may well be asked to find their own name card when they arrive and place it on a board or in a container.

► What activities are provided for the children as they arrive, and do they start working on them independently or with guidance? Look for puzzles, construction sets or books set out carefully in different parts of the room.

► Is there a good range of activities provided for the children? For example:

   – an area for creative and 'messy' activities

   – an area for early 'writing' activities and perhaps a computer

   – a role play area for dressing up and acting out different roles

   – an outdoor play area (well supervised) with climbing activities and bicycles

   – an area for sorting, matching and early number activities

► Do the children make the best use of the range of activities provided? Do they spend some concentrated time at one activity, perhaps supported by an adult, before moving on to the next activity?

► Is the relationship between the staff and the children productive? Most nursery staff aim to encourage children rather than direct them, but also have the strength of character to make sure that children do as they are asked.

► Are the children well-behaved as they move around the nursery? How are they spoken to by the staff?

► How are refreshments/lunches organised? Are hot meals available if your child stays all day?

► Can you see your own child settling into the nursery?

Printed information about a nursery is very often glossy and glowing, but how does it come across to you when you visit it during a normal busy morning?

Other key issues

The Department for Education and Employment (DfEE) offers guidance to nurseries about the policies they must have in place. Parents may wish to check that the following issues have been considered:

Health and safety

The nursery must provide a safe working environment for both children and adults.

▶ Do staff check all areas of the nursery and all equipment regularly to ensure safety?

▶ How is good hygiene ensured, if children are handling food or playdough for example?

▶ What are the security arrangements for the nursery? Who can gain access and how?

▶ What happens if your child is ill during the day?

Staffing

You need to check that the staffing levels in the nursery are of the right quantity and quality.

A state nursery school must have a qualified nursery teacher who will be in charge of the educational provision. In the best nurseries, the support staff will have a Nursery Nurse Education Board (NNEB) qualification which is a two year course recognised as providing the best preparation for working in a nursery. The ratio of staff to children should be 1:13 or better and, if younger children are in the nursery, the ratio should be increased.

A private nursery cannot call itself a nursery school unless it has a qualified nursery teacher in charge. The qualifications and experience of other staff are not regulated by law. However, many private nurseries have staff who are well qualified and experienced.

Behaviour

You will have been able to make a judgement about the standard of behaviour during your visit, but here are some more points you may wish to consider:

▶ Does the nursery have an official behaviour policy?

▶ How do the staff deal with poor or disruptive behaviour?

▶ How are parents involved, if their child's behaviour is poor?

▶ How is good behaviour rewarded?

Equal opportunities

You need to check how the nursery promotes equal opportunities for all its children.

▶ Do the staff meet the range of needs which the children have, regardless of race, culture, religion or disability?

▶ Does the nursery have the right resources to ensure that all pupils can take part in the full range of activities?

▶ Do the activities draw on experiences from different cultures, religions and festivals?

▶ Are girls and boys given the same opportunities? Are girls encouraged to play with construction toys? Are boys encouraged to spend time in the playhouse?

Special needs

Your child may have special needs or you may be concerned about the provision which is made should a special need become apparent. Children who have special needs may be 'statemented' (when a child is identified officially as having particular learning requirements) by the local education authority to ensure that they receive the support which they need.

▶ Is the nursery familiar with the Code of Practice for special educational needs? This ensures that children with special needs are fairly treated and given equal opportunities for learning.

▶ Does it have links with other agencies – eg. speech therapists – on which it can draw if a child has special needs?

▶ Are staff able to spot potential difficulties at an early stage?

▶ Is the nursery equipped to cater for children who have physical disabilities?

▶ How do children with special needs work and play alongside others?

Complaints

Another important area to consider is how your complaints, if you ever have any, would be dealt with. Find out from parents whose children are already at the nursery how complaints are dealt with and talk to the nursery staff themselves.

They should be dealt with:

– promptly   – thoroughly   – confidentially   – sensitively

After visiting possible nurseries, you should be in a good position to select the one which you feel will be best for your child. Of course, if you are in an area where nursery places are in high demand, the nursery may be selecting you! Make sure that you complete the application forms and have a clear understanding of the likelihood of being successful. You may wish to apply for a place in more than one nursery in areas where demand is high.

Chapter five

Starting at nursery – what you and your child can expect

A big step

Starting nursery is a big step for many children and their parents. It may be the first occasion on which your child has been away from your care for a substantial period of time, and this may be emotionally difficult at first.

Many children start nursery and take to it immediately. Try not to be hurt that your child does not appear to be missing you! Others take a little time to settle and need reassurance during the first few weeks. Often the parting time at the beginning of the session is the most difficult, and your child will settle very happily once you have left and his or her mind is on the activities of the nursery. A small number of children continue to be quite unhappy at nursery and you will need to discuss with the nursery teacher what you can do, if your child appears to be one of these.

> 'Young children's natural curiosity can be stimulated to help them learn effectively by providing novel first-hand experiences and opportunities to explore, investigate and solve problems.'
>
> *from* Teaching and Learning in the Early Years
> *(Penny Coltman and David Whitebread, Routledge 1997)*

Dos and don'ts when your child is starting nursery

One thing is for certain – the staff of a good nursery will have come across all types of children in the past, and making sure that they all feel secure and happy is a major part of their role.

Do take advantage of any opportunities to visit the nursery with your child before he or she starts full-time. Many nurseries offer induction sessions in the previous term so that your child can make a gradual adjustment to the new setting and new people.

Do talk to your child about starting nursery, being positive about the new activities in which he or she will be able to take part. If you can find a favourite activity on one of your visits, this will help to provide a focus for the child. Talking about nursery will help your child to come to terms with the change.

Do prepare your child for the personal tasks for which he or she will need to be responsible at nursery. Being able to go to the toilet unsupervised, dress, wash and dry face and hands unaided will all help your child to be more confident at nursery. If your child cannot tie shoe laces then he or she needs slip-on shoes. Skirts and trousers with elasticated waists may be easier than ones with buttons. If there are areas of personal hygiene about which you are concerned, discuss them with nursery staff.

If your child has been trained at home to tidy up toys and activities, then this again will help with settling in at nursery.

Do make sure that your child has plenty of sleep in the days leading up to starting nursery. New activities and new relationships will be tiring for your child and he or she needs to have a lot of energy and enthusiasm about them.

Do arrive on time before the first session (but not too early), help your child to remove clothing and to enter the nursery, guide them to an activity and, once your child appears to be settled, make a speedy withdrawal. Long goodbyes help no-one and if you cry your child may cry too.

Do be there promptly at the end of the session so that your child has the security of knowing that you have returned at the same time as all the other parents. Also, check your child knows what to do if you are ever delayed.

Do have a brief word with the nursery teacher to find out how your child has been during the session.

Do tell your child what you have been doing whilst he or she has been at nursery. It will help him or her to understand the concept of time passed.

Do discuss with the teacher any home circumstances that are relevant to your child: for example, a new baby, recent house move, family bereavement. It helps the teacher to understand and anticipate your child's needs.

Don't share your worries with your child. You may be anxious about how your child will cope with the change, but you should hide that anxiety or it will be quickly transferred to your child.

Don't pester your child about what they have been doing in the nursery. Many children prefer to keep their thoughts to themselves for a few days, or are tired, or simply do not remember. A young child is still sorting out lots of new experiences in his or her own mind. Sooner or later, your child will choose to share some of his or her experiences with you. You may just need to prompt a little!

Chapter six

The early years curriculum

When you walk into a secondary school classroom, it's easy to spot that education is taking place. You see a class of students, probably sitting at desks. You see a teacher, probably explaining a point or questioning a student. You quickly recognise the subject, even if you are not sure of the answers!

One of the features of the early years curriculum is that it is "messy". The classroom is not so structured. The curriculum is not easily separated out into subjects. The role of the teacher is far more subtle and not so obvious. Perhaps most confusing of all, lots of activities are happening at the same time, and it often seems as though children are simply doing what they want to do rather than what they need to do.

This section attempts to unravel some of the strands involved in the early years curriculum, so that you can understand what is happening and why. The starting point is to think about how children learn in their early years, because the education offered in good nursery schools, and other early years settings, is primarily concerned with maximising learning.

How do children learn in the early years?

The first seven years of a child's life is the period of most rapid physical and intellectual development. Children learn to walk and talk quite naturally, given the right conditions and lots of support and encouragement.

We know that if a language-rich environment is absent, children do not learn to talk. Equally, children with bi-lingual parents often learn two languages at the same time – a daunting prospect for any adult! It is the richness of the environment which encourages children's learning.

It is also clear that young children learn best by being actively involved – doing, exploring and finding out for themselves rather than being told. The young child may need a guide, someone to interpret experiences, someone to answer questions, someone to offer new words to describe what is happening. However, long explanations are likely to be too complex for the young child to understand.

No matter what your child is doing, whether it's painting, talking, shopping, singing or talking to you, he or she is probably learning from the experience.

Much research has shown that young children are not capable of thinking or learning in the abstract. They need to have **practical experiences** to support their learning. Try explaining to a four year old the way a television works. Of course they know what a television is, because they have seen one, and many young children can manipulate the remote control for the video with incredible dexterity, but the concept of radio waves passing through the air is abstract – not real enough for them to grasp.

Building on learning

Young children are like the rest of us in one respect. They start from what they know and gradually build on that knowledge and understanding. Young children need to learn in manageable steps, building on their existing experience. What children can already do rather than what they cannot do are the starting points for their learning.

Some children are packed full of confidence and will have a go at almost anything, sometimes with frightening consequences for parents! Some children are far more reticent and need lots of support and encouragement to attempt a new skill. Recognising that young learners are individuals, and ensuring that they are all given the confidence to progress and develop, is a key feature of a good early years curriculum.

Planning the early years curriculum

In planning the early years curriculum, teachers, nursery nurses and other adults take into account what they know about young children as learners.

A rich environment

When you go into a really good nursery school, you are immediately struck by the richness of the environment. It is interesting, whether you are five or fifty-five. There are lots of activities and it is colourful, attractive and inviting. Children entering such a nursery will automatically be drawn to something which interests them. But it is easy to forget that a great deal of planning has gone into making the environment so welcoming. The educators will have considered the quality of learning on offer. It is not all painting and playdough!

▶ There will be opportunities for children to 'read' attractive books comfortably and for them to 'write' with a variety of implements on a range of papers.

▶ There will be artistic activities, and a place for children to play creatively, maybe in a 'Post Office' or a 'shoe shop'.

▶ There will be construction materials, sand play and water play.

▶ Outside, there will be bicycles, wheelbarrows, balls, skipping ropes, hoops – in fact a whole range of equipment for play.

The list is never exhaustive, and is not meant to be, because the creative nursery leader seems to find a new activity just when the list is being finalised!

The right balance

It is not just the range of activities available at a nursery school which is important. It is also the balance. It is as important to have a table game involving counting skills as it is to make fairy cakes. Each offers a different set of opportunities for learning.

In the nursery, young children are rapidly building their knowledge of language, which will be one of the key tools for future learning. It is important that activities encourage children to communicate in a range of ways:

- talking, listening and discussion with others

- listening to stories and beginning to tell them themselves

- recognising that print carries meaning

- beginning early attempts at writing

Of course, the good nursery educator always makes sure that his or her contribution will enrich children's language skills: sometimes enforcing a particular idea or theme will be the focus; often a whole range of new knowledge and understanding will be produced by one single activity.

Good practice

Making mince pies

A group of six children are making mince pies with the teacher. The teacher first talks about the ingredients. Some of the children have not heard of lard before and the teacher explains what it is. All the children measure out their flour, with help, and sieve it into their bowls. One child laughs at the way the flour cascades from the sieve, and a few moments are spent talking about the way it looks like snow falling. Some of the flour is dusted where it should not be!

The ingredients for the pastry are added and gradually mixed, if rather sloppily. Lots more talk as the egg disappears into the mixture. When the pastry is rolled out, the children learn how to use flour to stop it sticking to the surface. Why does it stick? This too is discussed.

Pastry is cut out in circles for the pies. How many pies do you think you can make from your pastry? Later, the spare pastry is cut in a range of shapes to make biscuits. The children add some mincemeat, and a little decoration of pastry strips.

What will happen when the pies go in the oven? The children watch through the glass, see the pastry turning brown, and discuss the wonderful smells of baking pies.

Later in the day, everyone gets a pie with their milk and the children talk about what they have been doing. The teacher listens carefully to see how much they have learned.

Getting involved

In a good nursery school, the emphasis is on children being actively involved in a wide range of practical experiences. When they are not working closely with an adult, much of children's activity would be described as play. Because play is something adults tend to do when they are not working, its role in the education of young children has often been misunderstood and undervalued.

For young children, play is the natural way in which they find out about many things. Children:

- find out about relationships with others, how to share and cooperate

- develop their independent working skills

- have time to explore materials such as paint, sand, water and dough

- discover what they can build from construction kits

- can look at a range of books

Of course, children will only do this if the setting has been carefully organised to support their exploration and structure their play. It is also true that young children need to have their attention drawn to the important parts of their experience. Sometimes they will focus themselves and sometimes they need the support of an adult to help them focus. Nursery educators aim to make children's play purposeful rather than aimless, and they carefully observe what the children do.

> *In most nurseries, staff create a balance between supported activities and independent play.*

The session is structured so that there are a number of gathering times, bringing groups of children together for milk time, a story, or singing and music making. Each child will have certain tasks to complete during the session and times when they may choose from the range of other activities on offer.

In some nurseries, children are asked to plan their activities during the session, either orally or using pictures, so that their play is more purposeful. At the end of the session, children explain what they have been doing. This approach of **Plan … Do … Review** gives more structure to the child's activities and develops important skills of thinking forward, following a plan and recalling activities.

Whatever strategies the nursery uses, the aim of the staff will be to allow for pupils' individuality, whilst ensuring that their time is used most productively. And the nursery staff will be watching!

David's day

'When David arrived at nursery this morning he was not his usual self, and his dad did not have a clue what was wrong. Normally he comes straight into our main working area and goes to the large construction blocks which are his favourite activity. We have been watching him carefully on this activity and he is becoming much better at cooperating with other children. At first, he would not tolerate anyone else playing with him but, since Sara persuaded him to share the equipment a few weeks ago, he has realised that working with others can be fun. But this morning he seemed very sad. We persuaded him to try a painting and once he had started we left him to work on his own. He is using a wider range of colours now and his brush control is far better than it was.

By 9.30am David seemed much more cheerful and he joined one of the staff for a colour matching game. He knows a good range of colours now. After milk time, David went to the construction blocks and made a house. He worked very well with both Sara and Stephanie.

By 10.30am it was time for David to join a group making Easter cards. His cutting and sticking skills have developed really well since January, and he made the card virtually on his own. The big surprise was that he even wrote his name inside, because he has only written D in the past. We then went outside to play, and David was hurtling around like his usual self by this time. We looked around our garden and talked about the daffodils, some of which are in flower, others in bud.

By story time, David seemed very settled. He was keen to join in with some of the familiar parts of *The Ugly Duckling*. Maybe all the activity had taken his mind off his earlier worries.'

Keeping in touch

Nursery staff will always talk to parents and carers to find out as much as possible from the people who know the most. They will usually carry out their 'assessment' informally, by observing the child in the nursery. By talking with colleagues, nursery staff will gather a picture of the child's stage of development and this will provide a starting point. Many nurseries carry out regular observations of their children, keeping informal notes of significant developments. Some nurseries may have particular targets for some of their children.

All this information, carefully gathered, allows nursery staff to know roughly where children are in terms of their development. Of course, the real skill is to know where to take the child next, and this is where training as an early years educator, and experience, has taught staff the pattern of a young child's development.

Some steps may be easy: for example, if the child cannot yet count a small group of objects, then lots of activities involving counting will create the opportunity to build the skill. Some steps are harder: for example, if a child tends to dominate a play situation, the steps to ensure that he or she learns to share and cooperate may be more difficult.

Confidence

As children progress through the education system, they become more and more channelled into the demands of learning and of formal examinations. The early years curriculum has a freedom which helps teachers respond to children as individuals.

All young children are learning social skills, moral values and how to cope emotionally. They are also developing intellectual skills, knowledge and understanding. All these aspects of learning go hand in hand during a child's time in nursery.

Early years educators really do start from the idea that every child is different and, at age 3 or 4, there is no truer statement. Every child joining a nursery brings with them a wide range of prior experiences and has a unique personality, and this has to be responded to.

Above all, young children need the confidence to play and learn within the nursery setting, and it is only by promoting that confidence that they will be successful. Good nursery staff will always support children and have high expectations of what they can achieve. But they do not push them too hard. As every parent knows, this is often a difficult balance to strike.

Parents and nursery staff alike realise the vital importance of giving young children confidence in their own ability. They realise that praise for each success leads to more success.

Chapter seven

What your child should know by age 5

Desirable learning outcomes

All children must, by law, start school by the time they are five years old. To help guarantee high quality education for all pre-school children, there is a nationally agreed set of Desirable Learning Outcomes for children by the time they start school. All those involved in the education of pre-school children should be working towards these learning goals.

The goals have been agreed nationally to help parents and teachers have common expectations of what a child should be capable of achieving by age five. Staff in schools, playgroups and nurseries will be familiar with these expectations. Indeed, when nurseries and reception classes with four year olds are inspected, evidence that teachers are working towards the Desirable Learning Outcomes is the main yardstick for inspectors' judgements.

You will find these statements useful in assessing your child's progress, but you need to bear in mind that they are only 'a reasonable expectation for the average child'. Children's progress will be at different rates and individual achievement will vary.

How is your child doing? Is your child ready for school?

1. Language and literacy

Children should be able to:
- listen carefully and talk about their experiences
- use a growing vocabulary
- respond to stories, songs, rhymes and poems
- make up their own stories
- enjoy books and handle them carefully
- understand that words and pictures carry meaning
- understand that, in English, print is read from left to right and from top to bottom
- link sounds with words and letters
- recognise their own names and some familiar words
- know the alphabet and write their names correctly

3. Personal and social development

Children should be able to:
- show self-respect
- show respect for others
- work by themselves and as part of a group
- concentrate in their learning
- seek help when needed
- explore new ideas
- solve practical problems
- show independence in dressing and personal hygiene
- take turns and share fairly
- develop an understanding of what is right, what is wrong and why

2. Mathematics

Children should be able to:
- use mathematical language, such as 'circle', 'bigger', 'in front of'
- describe shape, positions, size and quantity, recognise and recreate patterns
- compare, sort and match using everyday objects
- recognise and use numbers up to 10
- be familiar with larger numbers from their everyday lives
- use mathematical understanding to solve practical problems
- understand and record numbers
- show early understanding of addition and subtraction, and use appropriate language

4. Knowledge and understanding of the world
Children should be able to:
- talk about where they live, their families and past and present events in their lives
- explore and recognise things in the natural world
- talk about why things happen and how things work
- explore a variety of materials, cutting, folding, joining and building
- use technology, including computers, to support their learning

5. Physical development
Children should be able to:
- move confidently and imaginatively
- show increasing control, coordination and an awareness of space
- use a range of small and large equipment for games
- use a range of equipment for balancing and climbing
- handle tools and materials safely and with increasing control

6. Creative development
Children should be able to:
- explore sound, colour, texture and shape
- respond in a variety of ways to what they see, hear, smell, touch and feel
- show their imagination through art, music, dance, stories and play
- show their ability to listen and observe
- use a widening range of materials, tools, instruments and other resources to express ideas

Baseline assessment

All children are assessed when they first start primary school. For most children, this will be when they join the reception class. Teachers use the term 'baseline assessment' because it marks the formal starting point for a child's school career.

Baseline assessment has two aims:

▶ To find out about what your child knows and can do, so that teachers can plan effectively for your child's learning needs.

▶ To help the school to measure and monitor your child's progress from when they start school, so that they can check whether your child is achieving his or her potential.

Schools can choose from a range of nationally agreed baseline assessment schemes. You will need to ask your child's primary school for details of the particular scheme which it operates.

Baseline assessment provides a clear starting point for your child's education at school. It helps you to know his or her current level of achievement in a range of skills. It allows you to judge how this compares with children of a similar age – make sure you do not compare your child with those who are in the same class but six months older! Perhaps most importantly, it helps both teachers and parents to know what a child needs to learn next.

Chapter eight

Supporting your child's early learning at home

Parents and educators

All parents want to help their child to learn new things. It is one of the pleasures of parenthood to watch your child gradually grow and develop, finding out more about the world and being able to achieve new successes. Most parents are good educators. It's often not being sure what to do which is most frustrating. The following pages offer you some ideas on how to help your young child.

> **How parents can help – five golden keys**
>
> ▶ Support your child with your time, not just in the early years, but throughout school life.
>
> ▶ Encourage early reading, writing and number skills at home – do not leave the nursery and the school to do everything.
>
> ▶ Encourage your child to feel positive about learning in general and about going to nursery or school in particular.
>
> ▶ Support your child as they tackle any new skills – a child needs to feel that learning a new skill is an opportunity not a threat.
>
> ▶ Listen to and talk with your child about his or her interests and experiences, including what they are doing at nursery.

Roots and wings

Praise **how** your child learns as well as **what** they have learnt: 'I liked the way you tried to use lots of colours in your picture'. That way, children begin to feel that trying hard is as important as a wonderful end result. They are then not afraid to try new things.

Being a good parent is all about giving your child roots and wings. Roots include a secure home life, basic codes of behaviour and basic skills. Wings are all about encouraging your child to develop his or her self-esteem and independence.

> *'Parenting is one of the most difficult jobs we will ever do, yet we have the least preparation for it. It helps to learn all we can about how children develop over the years, so that we can be the level-headed, understanding parent and caregiver that every child needs.'*
>
> *from* Family Matters: Have Realistic Expectations of Small Children *(Steve Duncan, Montana State University, 1998)*

How can I help with reading?

Choosing the right books

The following books are a selection from those that are nationally recommended and available in most bookshops. Choose ones which you think will suit your child's needs and interests.

What these books have in common is:

- simple vocabulary

- clear layout and typeface

- few words on each page

- interesting subject and setting

- pattern, rhyme and rhythm in the language

- attractive illustrations

- suitability for reading aloud with your child.

Title	Author	Publisher
Bet you Can't!	Penny Dale	Walker
Chatting	Shirley Hughes	Walker
Handa's Surprise	Eileen Browne	Walker
How do I put it on?	Shigeo Watanabe	Red Fox
I Love Animals	Flora McDonnell	Walker
Nandy's Bedtime	Errol Lloyd	Red Fox
On Friday Something Funny Happened	John Prater	Bodley Head
Ten, Nine, Eight	Molly Bang	Puffin
The Little Red Hen	Margot Zemach	Puffin
The Very Hungry Caterpillar	Eric Carle	Puffin

This list is just a starting point. There is a vast wealth of young children's fiction which you can share with your child. Try other books by the same authors or, once you have established the sort of stories your child likes, look for books with a similar theme. Don't forget to include some poems and rhymes. Remember to include some non-fiction books. It doesn't always have to be a story.

As you read through books with your child you will find that he or she begins to memorise some parts of the story – you won't be able to leave bits out! Encourage your child to join in reading with you because this is an important early stage in learning to read. Your child is building up a fund of reading knowledge which he or she will be able to apply when the time is right.

Let your child turn the pages. Discuss the pictures rather than rushing on with the story – they hold important clues to the meaning of the words. Begin to run your finger under the text so that he or she gradually recognises that it is the words which carry the meaning. Don't rush your child.

Hints for helping early readers

Working with letters

Make 26 small cards, each printed with a letter from the alphabet. Use lower case (small) letters. Can your child:

- pick out the letters which spell his or her name?
- recognise five letters by shape and sound?
- recognise ten letters by shape and sound?
- recognise all the letters by shape and sound?

Use the **sounds** the letters make rather than their name, ie. 'mmmmm' not 'em'. Try not to put a 'u' on the end of the sound, ie. 'mmmm' not 'muh'. This will help your child to use the sounds more effectively when hc or she begins reading.

If you use the five senses when reading, your child will learn more effectively:

- trace the shape of the letter
- say the sound of the letter
- draw the letter
- listen for the sound and pick the letter
- find things in the house which start with the sound of the letter

Pictures and sounds

Make picture cards (no words) for the words in bold type below. With a set of three cards, maybe more later, say the word and ask your child to point to the correct card. Then ask your child the following questions:

duck	bird	cup
▶ Which one begins with the 'b' sound?

car	fork	button
▶ Which one begins with the 'c' sound?

door	cat	ant
▶ Which one begins with the 'a' sound?

mouse	nest	book
▶ Which one begins with the 'm' sound?

There are lots of ways in which you can add to this game. With a few more cards you can play sound snap. With your letter cards you can match the letters to the picture cards.

More pictures and sounds

This time you need a set of picture cards where the letters at the ends of the words are matching and/or rhyme. Again, begin with a set of three cards, say the words and ask your child to point to the correct card. Then ask your child the following questions or similar ones:

bun	sun	cow
▶ Which two of these words sound the same at the end?

man	bat	hat
▶ Which two of these words sound the same at the end?

bee	pan	sea
▶ Which two of these words sound the same at the end?

boat	bed	coat
▶ Which two of these words sound the same at the end?

fish	dish	box
▶ Which two of these words sound the same at the end?

peg	key	leg
▶ Which two of these words sound the same at the end?

You can now develop examples of your own.

Does your child know these eight nursery rhymes? Practise saying each in turn. Can your child recite them?

▶ Sing a song of sixpence   ▶ Oranges and lemons

▶ Mary had a little lamb   ▶ Ding dong dell

▶ Rock-a-bye-baby   ▶ Ring a ring o'roses

▶ This little piggy   ▶ Tom, Tom, the piper's son

How can I help with writing?

Your child will start writing by drawing, colouring and 'pretend' writing.

You need to provide plenty of openings for your child to develop the manipulative skills which are essential for writing. Children who do not learn to hold and use cutlery cannot be expected to hold and use a pencil easily! So give your child a chance to develop good hand and finger skills through games and tasks around the home. Provide plenty of opportunities for drawing and colouring, using a range of crayons, coloured pencils and felt tip pens.

Note: if your child prefers to use his or her left hand for writing, do not try and change this. Left-handed children may need to slant the paper more than right-handed children, and particular attention needs to be paid to the child's pencil grip.

When you are doing some writing, involve your child. Make a list of things to buy at the supermarket and ask, 'Would you like to make a list?' You will often find that your child can make a pretend list of his or her own. The important lesson which this is teaching your child is that writing has a meaning and a purpose. Young children love making cards, so recycle Christmas and birthday cards and ask your child to write a message in them. You know that your child's first attempts will be 'pretend' writing, but ask him or her what they have written and offer lots of praise and encouragement.

The first word children learn to write is usually their name. Teach your child to write his or her name correctly, starting with a capital letter and the rest being lower case. Show your child how to form the letters correctly. Bad habits are far harder to correct than no habit at all, so it's worth taking the time to teach your child carefully.

Letts' *Pre-Schools Skills: Writing* contains guidelines on early writing skills.

Look around the home for different examples of print and illustration. Ask your child:

– to point to the words or writing on a cereal packet, toy box or magazine

– to point to the pictures

– to copy down some words

Alternatively, ask your child to cut out some words they know from a newspaper or magazine, and stick them on a piece of paper. Ask him or her to copy under the words on the paper. Make sure that you watch so that you can check that letters are being formed correctly.

My work, my writing

If your child draws a picture ask him or her to:

– write his or her first name on the back of the picture, so that you all know who it belongs to.

– write a word, or a few words, about the picture – 'Dad', 'shopping', etc. You may have to write the word for your child and ask him or her to copy it underneath.

Happy families

Ask your child to write down the names of your family and friends. Again, you may have to provide some of the names for your child to copy. Ask your child to write some part of the invitations for a birthday party.

Try to introduce writing as part of any activity which your child does at home.

How can I help with speaking and listening?

Children learn to speak and listen because they want and need to communicate. They want to make sense of the world around them. When they talk through their ideas, it often helps them to sort out their thinking. Young children copy the talk of those around them and, of course, some children grow up learning more than one language.

▶ Talk **with** your child, rather than just at him or her.

▶ Make sure some of your questions encourage more than one word answers.

▶ Talk about a range of subjects and experiences.

▶ Value what your child is saying.

▶ Listen to, rather than interrupt, your child.

▶ Make sure – with good eye contact – that your child **listens** when you speak.

How can I help with mathematics?

Sorting and matching

One of the early skills in mathematics is for a child to be able to sort items into groups. It doesn't matter what your child sorts, as long as he or she gets the practice. What about sorting fruits and vegetables or tipping out your cutlery drawer (no sharp knives, of course) and sorting the contents? Or sorting socks into pairs? Just be alert to the possibility, and lots of opportunities come to mind. Don't forget to count the items in the groups once they have been sorted. From sorting activities, children can begin to understand ideas such as 'more than' and 'as many as'.

Out and about

Take opportunities to spot numbers and to count when you are out and about. There is no better way to learn about numbers than in a real context. A visit to the supermarket offers endless openings. At first you might count out the apples or oranges but, in time, you should be able to ask your child to bring two bags of crisps and one bottle of orange juice. Don't forget zero, which often confuses young children. Make fun of it. 'Go and get me zero apples' is worth a try! Counting steps is always of considerable fascination for young children, because the physical rhythm of marching up or down is in time with the beat of the counting.

Playing board games

This is an old favourite, but you need to select games which lend themselves to counting. As well as the traditional spotted dice, why not try a dice with the digits 1 to 6 on the faces. This will be excellent practice for number recognition. It is quite possible to obtain dice with blank faces and, with the help of some stickers, you can make a dice with 5-10 on the faces. Young children often struggle with their starting point on a games board. You may have to remind them that the square after the one they have landed on is number one in their move. 'Which square do you think your throw will get you to?' is an interesting question to ask.

Playing cards

Playing cards is an invaluable game for practising a whole variety of mathematics skills. Snap is familiar to most adults, but there are variations on this theme in a range of matching and remembering games.

With four suits, and 1-10 in each suit, as well as the face cards, the game of snap is about counting, matching and sorting. Try a game of simple whist for starters. Deal five cards to each player. The first player lays any card and the other(s) have to follow suit. The player laying the highest card wins the trick.

Number cards

It is well worth making a set of number cards showing 1-10 because they can be used in a variety of different games and situations. If you put the same number of dots on the back of the card as the number on the front, a young child who can count to 10 can check the right answer. Here are some more ideas to try:

▶ Sort a tube of sweets into the various colours – eating is not allowed until the sorting is finished!
Can you match the cards to the size of the groups?

▶ Sort out small change: how many 1p, 2p, 5p and so on. Can you match the number to the group?

▶ Dominoes also provide excellent opportunities for counting, sorting and matching.

Once a young child can count, the next step is for them to be able to count a set no matter how it is arranged. It's amazing how many children can count a set of eight objects in a row, but are confused by the same objects arranged randomly. Does your child really know that the count always identifies the size of a group? They need to learn that the last number they say is the size of the set.

Extension activities

Children need a wide range of mathematical experiences – maths is not only about numbers! There are many openings for such activities at home:

▶ Discuss shapes of building bricks and toys – which are the circles, which are the squares?

▶ Compare the weight of two bags of sweets – which feels heavier?

▶ Discuss how much water or sand is held in different containers – how much water in the cup, is it full or empty?

▶ Compare the length of toys – which is longer, which is shorter?

▶ Talk about time – what time do you go to bed, when do you have lunch?

Most important of all, keep using the language of mathematics: 'How many?' 'Are there more?' 'Go three forward,' 'I have fewer than you.' Language is the vehicle for all learning. Mathematics is no exception.

Summary

How children learn - five golden keys

▶ A child's concentration is limited – learning should be broken down into short sessions with regular breaks.

▶ Children learn when they feel relaxed and supported by those around them.

▶ Children learn when they can see 'what's in it for them' – targets set need to be achievable within a reasonable time.

▶ Children learn in different ways, using all their senses – music, rhythm, role play, games and TV all need to be used alongside paper and pen.

▶ Children transfer knowledge from short term to long term memory when they review what has been learnt, often using visual clues and combining words and music.

How does the brain learn? Both sides of the brain control different functions and skills. The left side controls language, mathematics, logic and sequences. The right controls spatial ideas, music, images and imagination. Children and adults learn effectively when both sides of the brain are linked together. Activities that bring together, for example, language and music or mathematics and images will help your child learn more effectively.

Why parents matter most The government has made education one of its priorities. At the heart of its drive to raise children's achievements is a focus on the basic skills of literacy and numeracy. Targets have been set for all children to be able to read, write and handle numbers confidently by the time they leave primary school.

These targets will not be achieved just in schools. What happens to children in the early years – particularly at home – is decisive. You can play a major part in preparing your child to develop his or her early skills. Looking ahead to your child's achievements and school test results at ages 7, 11, 14 and 16, working at home with your child now will largely shape those achievements.

Authors' note We hope this book has given you some useful advice about the vital part you and your nursery school teachers play in your child's learning. Please write to us at Letts if you have any thoughts for this book's future editions.

32